"Grandma, You Already Am Old!"

Marlene Oxender

"Grandma, You Already Am Old!"

Volume Three in the *Picket Fences American Family Series*

Copyright © 2025 by Marlene Oxender

My work may be freely used but only by noncommercial users. It may not be adapted or changed in any way, and I must be given credit as the author.

Please feel free to contact me at mpoxender@gmail.com and check out my website: www.dottingmyteas.com

The antique desk clock on the front cover of this book once belonged to my Grandpa and Grandma Imm. The clock is a Big Ben De Luxe and was manufactured in the 1920s.

After my younger brother Stevie Kimpel passed away on March 1, 2024, I began noticing the number "eleven," which I now refer to as my "angel number." I chose to place the hands on the face of this desk clock at eleven minutes past eleven.

You may find my essay "Eleven Eleven" at www.dottingmyteas.com

ISBN: 979-8-9924615-0-3

Cover photo credit: Jamie McCann, Auburn Art Gallery, Auburn, Indiana

DRL Press, Georgetown, Texas

Contents

Introduction 5

Good Morning, Moon 7

My Grandmother's Handwriting 15

About My Mom 23

My To-Do List 35

Treasure Hunting 43

Thank You 49

An Amaryllis Kind of Grandmother 55

Baby Toes 61

A Baby Toes Prayer 75

Being a Grandmother 81

This Year's Model 87

The Grandmother in My Mirror 97

Dear Younger Me 103

Country Roads 107

So What's Your Superpower? 115

Over-the-Top 121

Sleep Tight 133

Postscript 137

Now the End Again 139

Introduction

Blessed are those who don't know they are old, for it will be a child who will tell them so.

Grandparents everywhere know how young they are, and they mentally need to hang on to that idea. No cute little kid needs to tell us otherwise.

It was my four-year-old grandson, who gets around like a monkey most of the time, who reminded me of my oldness. There were even witnesses who heard his words after I asked him if he would continue to visit Grandma and Grandpa when we're old.

There was a short moment of silence before he answered: "Grandma, you already am old."

What happens when you're a grandmother and a writer of stories? A book about oldness gets put together. The sorry thing is, I'm a nonfiction writer. Everything I write is true. And I have enough words to fill a book about all the oldness going on around me.

The secret that we older people know about staying young – is in not recognizing that we're old. We don't need that kind of negativity.

But we do need to spend time with young people who innocently, yet gladly, remind us that we've celebrated more than a few birthdays.

Good Morning, Moon

Those of us who are up and about early in the morning know what a peaceful time of day it can be. Sometimes the morning moon and I spend time together as I sit at my computer and type.

When I notice a bright little spot in the sky, I look to see if the moon really is peeking in through the west window. I find myself saying, "Well, good morning, Moon." And though I say no more, certainly the moon can feel my thoughts and know it's looking awfully pretty.

There it is, hovering in the sky, letting me know it has returned for an early morning show. Sometimes there is a cloud cover – in many shades of grey – moving back and forth and adding to the beauty of the morning skies.

Then there is the east window where I know the sunrise will be happening soon. The skies transform from dark to a shade of blue, sometimes periwinkle blue. Then shades of pink appear before a golden yellow mixes in, and the sun makes its cameo appearance.

I remind myself it's the real thing. If I were an artist, I would paint a picture of the happenings in the morning skies.

It's a wonderful feeling not knowing which way to look. The sun is in the east, and the moon is in the west. Shall I watch the sun appearing or the moon disappearing? All I know is, I am watching some magnificence going on.

The need to tell my friends overcomes me, and the texting to those who are early risers begins. It's as if I know something they don't, and I must share it so they don't miss out.

My husband's Grandma Parnham, like most grandmothers, was an early riser. Those who knew her would tell of her pie-baking skills and the fact that a warm pie was something that came out of her oven in the early morning hours.

We live in a small town, and the locals knew Grandma was the pie-baker at The Yankee Pancake House, a restaurant so close to her home it didn't matter that she never drove a car.

It was always fun to hear people of her generation tell me they visited the restaurant just to enjoy a piece of her homemade pie. I should have asked them what kind of pie they ordered. Was it butterscotch?

A friend once told me that Grandma Parnham's name is so cute, it should be on the front of a children's book. I agree – there's a book waiting for me to write.

When I asked my husband what his favorite childhood memory was, I already knew the answer. I just wanted to hear him say it. He spent a lot of time with his Grandma Parnham and knew his way around the old barn. It seems he knows more Lawrence Welk trivia than a guy ought to know. But he has nothing but good memories of times spent in her little country home.

Farmers don't need a text from their friends telling them to look for the moon. Without a doubt they notice the sky as they pull a little morning air deeply into their lungs on their walk to the barn.

Grandma Parnham's way of life always looked so simple. Doilies in place upon the furniture inside her home. Heirloom plants in the landscaping outside. A barn that makes you ask what year it was built, for it seems it has been there forever.

I wonder how many kitty-cats were born in that barn and claimed it as their home, a place where they could tumble and play with their siblings.

When I turned fifty, I remember making a decision that I was going to have the best decade imaginable. I had become a grandmother at the age of forty-seven. My husband and I were empty nesters. The decision to have the best decade ever seemed so simple. Very logical. I now laugh as I look back at the years behind me and all the changes in the world.

On the morning of my fifty-ninth birthday, I was awake early and typing away at my computer. Out of the corner of my eye, I noticed a bright light peeking through the window at me.

I looked closer and asked, "Is that you, Moon?"

As the cloud cover was making the moon appear then disappear, I felt I should quit typing and pay attention to my first gift of the day.

When there's a vase of fresh flowers in my home, I make a habit of letting them follow me around for the day. It seemed the perfect moment to move my birthday flower arrangement from the dining room table to my desk.

The moon, relentless in its beauty, continued to peek into the window as I sat at my desk. And I could feel the charm of the flowers beside me. White roses and white daisies. Red alstroemeria, tiny green mums, and pretty berries. A reminder we were thought about and loved as the world was being created.

No matter the date and year of our birth, we were put on this earth to live our own life and times – no one else's. We experience our own set of sunrises and sunsets. Our own set of problems. Our own set of joys.

I remember hearing that life on earth was going to pass by quickly, and I would someday know what it is like to be a young girl living in an older body.

Indeed, I found it is true. We look into the morning mirror, and our reflection is peeking back at us. It's the real thing, and we would never ask an artist for a painting of what we are seeing.

It may be that our hair has taken on various shades of grey. With silver and white highlights. Or a pretty shade of periwinkle blue.

After we ask who that person in the mirror is, we need not say more. We simply need to wake up a bit and come to our senses. There are good thoughts waiting for their turn.

As my birthday continued, I received an afternoon knock upon the door. My friend Marcy handed a gift bag to me where I found a small carved angel with flowers in her hands. Just the right words are inscribed upon her dress. I set my new little angel girl on my desk, where she will always be in my peripheral vision.

Later in the day my grandchildren called me, and I heard them sing the Happy Birthday song. It made me notice that even the birthday song changes over the years. Long ago they sang to "Marlene." Then they sang to "Dear Mom." Now it's "Dear Grandma."

My birthday ended on a perfect note (pun intended) when I opened an email to find yet another note before heading to bed. There within Deedee's email was something I had never received before: a birthday poem written just for me.

Having another birthday really does change our interests and the way we spend our days. We plan road trips to flower shops and used book stores. We mosey through antique malls that dare display toys from our childhood. We ask where the place is that serves the best homemade pie. Some of us will order butterscotch.

As the person peeking back at us in the morning mirror appears to be taking on changes with each passing year, perhaps all we need to recognize is the magnificence that is going on. We're becoming the person we were intended to be, inside and out.

And we are loved – as far as the east is from the west.

A view of the Christmas morning moon on December 25, 2023, from a west window in our home.

My Grandmother's Handwriting

I imagine nearly all of us own a box of items we plan to keep. The box is often tucked away in an attic or closet, and it holds little treasures that bring back memories from long ago.

It would be fun to throw a "Box Party" and tell everyone to bring their box. We would take turns lifting the items from within and telling the story behind each one. Old love letters would certainly be the most interesting, but I'd settle for a greeting card or two.

My Grandma Imm signed her cards "Grandparents Imm." I remember receiving a white purse as a birthday gift from her and Grandpa one year. The purse was so fancy, I probably only carried it to church, so it is still in perfect condition. I wonder where she purchased it.

Then there is the hinged recipe box found in nearly everyone's kitchen. When we read a recipe card with a handwritten list of ingredients, we are reminded that a special person in our life had taken the time to share something good from their own life. More often than not, they've written their name on the upper right-hand corner of the card.

The electronic world has made it easy to share recipes at the touch of a button, and the next generation will likely no longer need a place to store their written recipes.

I, however, still use the little wooden recipe box my husband made for me years ago. It's fun to thumb through, as it takes me back in time. There are recipes from old friends and neighbors as well as from people I've worked with over the years.

I found my Grandma Imm's handwriting in a 1958 children's book *The Lookies*, which is a publication for the World Book Encyclopedia.

The book was divided by the months of the year. In the month of February, Grandma wrote answers to the questions about President Washington and President Lincoln: Did Washington and Lincoln help others? She wrote, "yes." Would you like to help others? She wrote, "yes." How would you do it? She wrote, "beats me." At least she was honest.

If Grandma were to spend a day with me, and I gave her a tour of my house, would she be surprised to learn there is no sewing machine in my home? Would she ask where my embroidered dresser scarves are? I would have to show her the two embroidered scarves I own and ask her if she remembers having stitched them so many years ago.

I would talk to Grandma about those bread wrapper rugs she crocheted. I loved the crunchy sound when they were stepped on and the feel of them beneath my bare feet. I can only wish Grandma would have taught me to crochet. She knew how to embroider and tat. I wonder how many children she shared her talents with.

Grandma would likely marvel at today's appliances and cars. She would wonder where my huge garden is and ask to see the root cellar. I would show her the glass cookie jar that once belonged to her.

I would ask Grandma if we could take a short drive and spend the day together at Sauder Village in Archbold. She would likely feel very much at home. It would take a lot of time to stroll through the museum as she told me how things were back then.

Grandma would likely ask why ladies are dressed the way they are these days. I would tell her that by today's standards, she would certainly be considered a fashionable lady who looks very put together – a "fashionista" they may call her. Pictures from long ago reveal just how cute she really was. I would tease her about the tiny waistline she managed to hang on to all the days of her life.

Grandma and I would likely spend some time going through her box of letters that date back to the early 1900s, and I would read the letters to her and ask her to tell me more.

She was around when serious family farming was going on. When the men gathered in the fields for a day of threshing, and the women cooked the meals. She was a young lady during two world wars and became a grandmother who found out what it was like to send four of her oldest grandsons off to the service.

After a conversation such as that, I would tell Grandma that life on earth sometimes seems so odd to me. I would not ask her why life is full of so many ups and downs and highs and lows, for I know she may answer with, "Beats me."

My guess is she would tell me I am catching on with each passing year. If I told her how many mistakes I've made, would she tell me everyone makes a boatload of mistakes?

Maybe she would tell me life on earth doesn't offer a brand new start, but it does offer a chance for a brand new ending.

Grandma may likely tell me what matters is how gently we lived. How giving we were. How gracefully we let go of the burdens we were not meant to keep. How words never meant to take up residence in our heart need to be allowed to fly away.

Would she tell me I am being held like when I was little? That none of us are really alone? That we can close our eyes and feel the embrace of our grandparents and those who've loved us?

Three of my grandparents held me when I was a baby, but I was never held in the arms of my Grandpa Kimpel. He passed away just weeks before my parents were married. I imagine he would have held his grandchildren very tightly, just as my dad did with his grandbabies. Grandpa would have lifted me and held me as his sons did.

Our grandmothers never saw the age of electronics. They never heard a child say, "Hey, Grandma, turn it off and turn it back on again, and see if it works."

Our grandparents knew that people work better when they unplug for a while. They knew to be outside, walk barefoot, and embrace the dirt. They delivered their babies at home. They prepared homemade meals and gathered around the supper table. They enjoyed time on their front porch – just breathing. They loved each other, and they loved their families.

My mother didn't keep just one box of sentimental and

important items that have become conversation pieces for the rest of us. No, not just one box. Maybe 50 boxes. Maybe 100. But who's counting?

Those who sort through collections of saved stuff will undoubtedly find a few handwritten recipes and will cherish the handwritten part. They may never use the recipe, but they will indeed marvel at their grandmother's handwriting.

We know we "can't take it with us," but can we take our talents? Is there crocheting and tatting in our next life?

If it's true we take with us the things we've stored in our heart, then our hearts need an ongoing purge of the negative things we "Daresn't ought to keep," as our grandparents would have said.

It's a funny thing: Just when we think we have shooed away negative thoughts, we find they've welcomed themselves back in again.

When we sort through our box of memories, we may ask if the items within are things we should let go of or something we should keep.

We should remember how wonderfully we're made. Beautiful eyes and funny noses. Strong hands. And the little box within our hearts that has a way of letting us know there's more room.

We don't have to look far to see how much we're loved. It starts with the sunrise and doesn't end at sunset. The moon and the stars have taken their place, just for us. Sometimes the crescent moon is golden; sometimes it is white. There are times we see the moon's face and laugh as we tell others we really did see its funny nose the other night.

And those beaches. The feel of the sand beneath our bare feet. The sound of the waves crashing in. Customized moments. The seashells, just an arm's-length away. A souvenir the world will send home with us.

We know we leave good memories on this earth, but do we take memories with us? Memories of hard work and restful days. Memories of the good feelings after helping others. Memories of growing older and not knowing all the answers. Memories of simply answering with the truth when we say: "beats me."

FEBRUARY PRESIDENTS

Who is in charge of your schoolroom?.. Your teacher is in charge. Your father and mother manage your home. Perhaps you lead your class in grades. So, you know what a leader is.

What is the man called who is leader of our country? (P-6559) *Washington*
Do you know who is President now?.. *yes*
February is the birthday of two great Presidents (F-2503). Who were they? *Lincoln, Washington*
What is a "great" man? Does it mean size? ....*Lincoln*..................
Does it mean goodness?...........Does it mean helping others, or hurting them?
....
Did Washington and Lincoln help others? ...*yes*..........................
Would you like to help others? *yes*.
How would you do it? *beats me*.

FEBRUARY BIRTHDAYS

TO BE REMEMBERED

About My Mom

It seems the month of May is when the busyness begins. Gardening tools make their way out of the back shed. Flowers decide it's time to bloom. Ballgames begin.

We have reason to stop what we're doing and head to dance recitals, musicals, and graduation parties. The older I get, the more I appreciate speaking with young graduates and asking what they hope their tomorrows will bring.

Warmer weather often brings afternoon rainstorms which you would think could dampen our spirits, but the opposite often happens. The air feels wonderful, and the sound of thunderclaps can be enjoyable.

For my family, another big event was our youngest brother's birthday. When you have Down syndrome, you celebrate your birthday. Stevie proudly announced which birthday was upon him, and those around him – whether he knew them or not – learned how old he was going to be. There was no such thing as too many presents or too many greeting cards. Stevie would let it be known there would be cake, and there would be ice cream.

My mother celebrated ninety-two birthdays. I guess you could say the same thing happened to her – she let people know how old she was. She believed after the age of ninety, you should include the "half" in your age. So really, Mom lived to be ninety-two and a half.

In the spring of 2019, my siblings traveled home to celebrate Stevie's fiftieth birthday in our old high school gymnasium. We were together with many friends and family. Pictures were taken. Food was eaten. Hugs were given.

It was work getting that party ready, but it ended up being a relaxed and fun afternoon with so many people stopping in to wish Stevie a happy birthday. More than a few commented how it was fun watching Mom have such a wonderful time. It seemed she thought the party was for herself.

Just three days following the big celebration, her family gathered in the emergency room after she experienced a stroke.

Life was immediately different. We always knew the day would come when Stevie's brothers and sisters would be taking care of him. And there we were. We had fifty years to prepare for it, but I remember the feeling of it happening so suddenly.

Mom's funeral services were a week later, and I realized I had time to write about my mother. So I did. My cousin Collene read the following at the funeral home for me:

"This past Sunday morning, I was replying to an email from out-of-town friends who had sent their condolences to me regarding the loss of my mother.

"I was telling them my mom was a 'writer' and had written stories about others' lives when it occurred to me possibly no one had written a story about her life.

"Mom passed away on a beautiful Friday night – in the home she had lived in for seventy years. She had raised eleven children in that home.

"And all of us know her children turned out to be fairly good people – with Stevie proving to us he is the 'grand finale.'

"In recent months, I have been putting together a gratitude journal for myself. In that journal, I have placed copies of black-and-white family photos that were taken in the 1960s.

"In a photo dated April of 1963, my Grandpa Imm, my siblings, and the Imm cousins are gathered around the same dining room table that can still be found in my parents' home.

"Grandpa Imm was celebrating his sixty-eighth birthday. There are candles on his cake. I was a baby, and my cousin Kathy was holding me. It's great fun for all of us to find those cousin photos and identify who is who.

"Last Tuesday, at the age of ninety-two and a half, my mom baked yet another birthday cake. She was ready for Stevie's actual fiftieth birthday.

"It is anyone's guess how many birthday cakes my mom must have baked in the seventy years she lived in that home. And how many candles did she place on the cakes she had so lovingly put together?

"My mother did not need to Google anything – she had a set of encyclopedias at her fingertips. We now know it was well worth the financial investment she and Dad made in order to purchase that set of books. Mom and her children used those books to look up many things over the years.

"She never stopped using those encyclopedias.

"After she passed away and before we even called the hospice nurse, it occurred to me there is a photo of me as a newborn taken in December of 1962. It was a picture of Mom and me in the very same spot where I was standing beside her hospital bed.

"Mom was thirty-six years old when I was born. I was her ninth baby. In the photo, she is in a rocking chair. She was wearing a plaid dress, and she was holding me in her arms. I was wrapped in a baby blanket, of course. Her set of encyclopedias can be seen in the background, and a Christmas crèche is on a shelf. My baby bed is also in the background.

"And there we were in the same corner of the house.

She in a hospital bed. And I was taking care of her.

"The decision to take her home with hospice services was made on Wednesday of last week when the hospital social worker told us we needed to transfer Mom to an inpatient hospice unit or take her home.

"We decided that she – and all of us – needed to go home.

"So on Thursday afternoon, she was transferred by ambulance to her home. As she was being wheeled from the ambulance to her front door, she lifted her hand in the air. It was a joyful wave to her children who were there to walk with her into the house. Her arms could also feel the beautiful spring air that day.

"Stevie was even present, and he was hoping Mom would 'get better' as she always did in the past – after any of her hospitalizations.

"Mom let us know in so many ways she wanted to be home for just one more day. Her family was so important to her, and she was able to have a few more moments with some of those she loved.

"My mom and dad, as well as our aunts and uncles, have taught us that the making of memories is truly a priceless gift. Their generation knew how to do things. How to garden. How to can food. How to sew. How to fix things. They even knew how to make maple syrup. They knew how to square dance. How to keep bees. How to go fishing and how to farm.

"Our sweet memories have taught us to remember how important it is to spend time with family and to cherish our friendships with others.

"Every day of our life is a chapter in our book. We too can make it a best seller."

• • •

A month after Mom passed away, I took Stevie to an appointment with his chiropractor. While we were sitting in the waiting room, a woman who was probably in her fifties walked through the lobby with her mother. The mother needed to watch her step, so the two were holding hands. They were both smiling. And they made me smile. Until I cried.

Just a few weeks prior, I was holding my own mother's hand, and we were walking in the same lobby.

The two will never know they made me cry. And it made me wonder if at sometime in the past, the sight of my mom and me together ever made another woman cry.

Perhaps the grieving we continue to do after we have lost a loved one – is just the love we want to keep giving, but can't.

The last time my mom held my hand was a week before she passed away when we were posing for family photos at Stevie's birthday party.

I remember the last phone call I picked up from her. She wanted to discuss what we were going to do on Stevie's birthday. Of course we didn't know we were going to be spending the evening of his birthday in the emergency room.

I don't think I took my relationship with her for granted, yet I have heard myself say, "We always think we have tomorrow."

In the later years of my mother's life, she received flowers from her children after we decided to remember her on our own birthdays. Those who made the deliveries from the local flower shop told us it was fun to spend a few minutes with her. She knew the flowers were from the child who was having a birthday. She often didn't know how old we were but could do the math if she wanted to.

Mom knew we would cry after she was gone. But through our tears, we know we did a few things right. We sent flowers to her while she was still alive. We drove home to see her. We knew she needed to know she was loved and cared for.

Many of us look back at Stevie's big day and realize Mom had unknowingly arranged her own going-home party. She was able to embrace her friends and family one last time.

When we think of those who have gone before us, do we remember they had special people in their lives they held dearly? Did we hear them ask who will take care of a loved one they are leaving behind?

Do the people I love know I love them? Have they heard me say I wish a beautiful life for them even after I walk no more on this earth?

My grandchildren will know their grandmother's favorite word was "cherish." They will know it not only because I wrote about it, but they are going to feel it as they grow up. And in all probability, your grandchildren will know the same.

The flowers sent to us in the spring of the year certainly speak a message. If a card were attached, we would clearly read, "Hey, I love you. Hope you enjoy the flowers. Go find a vase. Show them off for a few days. Love you always."

The blossoms around us continue through the autumn months as the landscaping is changed in such a beautiful way – another sign we are genuinely loved.

Then the winter months begin. The snowflakes can make us feel as if we live in a snow globe. We're designed to withstand a few snowballs while we make snowmen with those we are growing up with. And we figure out how to go sledding on the hills that are sometimes within walking distance of the home we're growing up in.

Mom embraced the life that was given to her. She was

given eleven children to raise – eleven little souls to cherish, nurture, and love. She did the best she could do with the knowledge she had. Her encyclopedia set was the closest thing to online learning at that time.

Mom simply did not want to do much reading in the later years of her life, so she left the studying up to me and went the "natural" route with her health. At the age of eighty-seven, she embraced new approaches to stay healthy. She was a braggart when it came to how well she felt. I often heard her tell others she didn't have an ache or a pain anywhere.

Those who live past the age of ninety often prove there are ways to care for those around them. Through their love. Through their encouraging words. Mom said if you are still in your eighties, you are a youngster.

We are here to love ourselves as well as others. To make somebody else's life better. Age does not get us out of the work we are meant to do. So get busy – oh you who are still youngsters – you have a lot of living to do!

A family photo taken on May 18, 2019, at Stevie's 50th birthday party.
Front row, left to right: Elaine, Marlene, Ruth, Stevie, and Carolyn.
Back row, left to right: Ed, Lee, Jeanette, Darrell, Jayne, and Don.

My To-Do List

I went and did this thing called "getting a little older."
It seems everyone is doing it.
It's certainly not a fashion statement –
this thing called getting older

But I can't help it.

On my birthday last year I happened
to ask of my husband,
"What's up?"

He said it was my age
and laughed at how funny he can be.

So I ventured down the road on a sunny December day
out and about on my birthday – a habit I won't break.

I moseyed through favorite stores
so beautiful in holiday décor.

My spirit was revived a bit.
My shopping bags were full of gifts.

Time to head home
and find some ribbons and bows.

My husband, so helpful,
met me at the door
and kindly asked,
"What's up?"

A wonderful moment to go ahead and tell him –
"Oh dear, it's your credit card bill!"
and I laughed at how funny I can be.

Moments later I found my shopping list
right there upon the desk.

My own handwriting
letting me know there's stuff I
should have bought.

And what's this –
the to-do list I had jotted?

Poor little thing. Neglected indeed.
Did the phone just ring?

My friend says she needs to stop over.
"Oh yes, but won't you please wait just a minute?"

The cleaning fairies are mysteriously full of energy
and lickety-split fast when they need to be.

The spirit within me cannot be fooled
into thinking you'll soon be over.
I really need a friend who'll kindly give me notice.

I say to myself, "Oh, I'm having company?"
and my legs move faster than ever.

My mind makes decisions rather quickly.
The dishes find a spot in warm, soapy water.
The dustcloth makes a high-speed appearance.
The sweeper turns on, and the laundry is sorted.

My imaginary pocket watch
as pleasant as can be.
From room to room he follows me.

His hand ticks gently forward
but only once per second.
When time's up, the doorbell chimes –
Those eight familiar musical notes
as pretty as can be
kindly informing my friend is at the door.

We'll sit and talk and just be together.

What do you mean when you say you can't stay?
Don't you want to see how the cleaning fairies
just made my day?

Stay a few minutes; I'll give you a tour.
Surely don't tell me you'd find it a bore.

Well, if you're heading out, so am I.
Let's go on a road trip and find some homemade pie.
We'll laugh as we talk about the messiness of life.

We can reminisce.
Remember our childhood dreams?
Some of them came true after all!

Although "get older" was never on our to-do list,
it's something that happened before we could know it.
The dusting of baseboards made the list.
The windows and house need a huge powerwash.
The car needs waxed,
and the landscape doesn't clean itself.
And, oh, that garage!

If I were to live my life once again,
with a rake in my hand and old shoes on my feet,

I'd sing and whistle with no feelings of defeat.

The outdoor air – a gift from above.

Butterflies and starlings are decorating my yard,
and I just scared a chipmunk caught off guard.

I found the craziest bug there ever could be.
Come over here quickly so you can see!
A loud clicking noise – is he a click beetle?

With sun on my shoulders and pen in my hand,
it's time to sit down and write while I can.

The wonderment of life. Who knew?

How many more beetles are out there to find?
Moths and dragonflies are now on my mind.
Life is full of work, and life is full of play.
Can we take our work and make it into play?
If that's something I can do, please sign me up.

My hands may turn wrinkly from all that water
and my knees will speak up with an old familiar creak
but somewhere inside me, I can find a song.
I'll carry a tune in that proverbial old bucket.
If the birds can sing, so can I.

Here we are, just passing through
yet easily held captive by treasures on earth.
Serendipitous moments:
the universe speaking in present tense.

Living in the here and now –
earth really is a big playground!

Moments to play and moments to rest.
Moments we're just trying to do our best.

Custom-made moments.
Who knew?

Surely we'll know when our earthly work is done.
We'll freely ascend and meet up with old friends.

We'll speak of the wonders of life,
the ways to explore and learn even more.

How easily love is given and received in return
by letting each moment have its own turn.

It's like packing a suitcase full of kindness –
a suitcase we'll leave behind.

Our virtues we'll take with us.

An earthly to-do list?
Magnificent indeed.

Penny Musser took this photo of a monarch butterfly during a hospice memorial service in 2010. Penny and her sister Peggy were friends of mine, and I cherish this photo.

"GRANDMA, YOU ALREADY AM OLD!"

Treasure Hunting

When I was a child, it seemed as if it took forever for a year to pass by. I would hear older people talk about how quickly time flies, and I didn't know how they could say such a thing. Certainly they knew how long it took for Christmas morning to get here.

In my mind, anyone who looked like a grandparent or had white hair would have to admit they've been around for a long, long time. Part of their testimony would be that it took ages for them to get to be so old.

Then adulthood happens, and we end up turning the pages of our calendars just as quickly as we were told. We watch our children meet all the milestones and grow up and graduate. Then the college years. Then weddings. Then grandbabies.

When my grandchildren were ages two through six, I remember telling others that I want to bottle them up and keep them just as they are. Life is good when children are around.

Anyone who knew my brother Stevie knows he was in love with babies. He had to accept that they grow up, and then he was left looking for a new baby to hold. A friend of mine recently asked if those with Down syndrome connect at an even greater level with the energy a baby has to offer. What is it about babies that comforts us so much?

We watch babies grow up and start playing with toys that help them get their work done. Construction trucks and hard hats for boys. Toy kitchens for girls.

Adults can be in awe of the things children want to know and how eager they are to be involved in what's going on. I've never looked at a water tower and wondered how it works, but my grandsons have asked for an explanation.

Children are great at making suggestions about what to do next. My grandson Deano shared an idea that gained traction when he asked: "Hey Grandma, how about you be the kind of grandmother who hides candy, and I will be the kind of grandson who finds it?"

What a reminder – all of us will be remembered by how we lived our life. By the choices we made. By what we held dear.

Our friends can describe us by finishing a sentence: The kind of person who... The kind of friend who... The kind of grandparent who...

I already know I am the kind of grandmother who gets down on the floor and plays board games and puts puzzles together. I've also been told I spend a lot of time at the computer keyboard. Apparently I'm a master typist, and Deano has done a wild impression of me showing how fast I can type. Apparently I look up occasionally before I go back to rapid typing. He's the kind of grandson who makes others laugh.

I remember before my fiftieth birthday, I joked that I had no plans of informing my body that I was turning fifty. Everyone knew the best birthday I could have was a very quiet one.

Having not told my body how old it now is, I was a bit on the surprised side when it told me. It happened in the middle of an afternoon when I was on the living room floor. I wanted to do a somersault, and I couldn't do one.

There I was on the floor. Alone with no witnesses. Easy peasy. Just do a somersault. I was in disbelief when I did not quickly roll forward. A moment in time such as that makes a person go into problem-solving mode. No need for disbelief. I wondered if I should get myself on the couch and launch from there. That didn't work either. My attempt at a somersault turned into me just sitting on the floor. I continued to think; certainly I would figure it out. Arms on the floor. Shoulders forward. But no go.

It seems so simple, even as I type this. Just do a somersault. I told my daughters about this new little problem of mine, and they told me to just do one. I told them I can't. It's not that easy.

I asked my young friend Stephanie, who is in her thirties, if she could still do a somersault. She told me she assumed so but hadn't tried to do so in years.

I told her one of my regrets is not doing a somersault every day of my life. Doesn't that make total sense? You would not lose your ability. If you can do a somersault today, then certainly you can do a somersault tomorrow. Someone should have told me this years ago.

My great-nephew, Abram, recently asked me if I knew what yesterday's tomorrow is. It seems that riddles from a six-year-old always make us smile.

Today may be yesterday's tomorrow, but today is also the future I apparently didn't prepare my body for.

So as a public service announcement to young women everywhere: Start your morning out right with a somersault. Then you will never lose the ability.

A few weeks after I shared this advice with Stephanie, she sent a video of herself completing a somersault. I hope she always appreciates that little bit of shared wisdom.

In trying to meet my new goal of being the kind of grandmother who hides things for children to find, I brought a bag of little toys to a backyard family reunion.

Not knowing how I should conduct the hunt, I asked the six- and seven-year-old young men in my life if they could help me out. They told me it wasn't a problem at all and took care of hiding the organic candy suckers in the yard. There were bouncy balls from the dollar store and little blow-up beach balls. The boys took care of making sure every adult and child walked away with a prize.

It's a good thing young children can be left in charge of projects such as treasure hunts, for we adults have enough work to do.

Over the years, all of us have heard older people talk about the quirky things they do. Things like walking into a room and wondering what they walked in there for. And looking for their glasses only to find them on top of their head. The list goes on.

Then there is the kind of treasure hunt you don't know you are in. The kind where you find an item you forgot you had hidden in a special spot. Sometimes it ends with cash prizes.

The crazier this world seems to be, the easier it is for me to see where our treasures lie. A simple touch on the back somehow leaves us with a sense of comfort. Things like cuddle time with a purring kitten. Inviting the grandchildren over to spend the day. Going out to lunch with friends. Sharing newspaper clippings from 1952.

Way back when I completed my last somersault, I didn't know it was my last somersault. Life is full of so many last times we didn't know would be the last time.

We're alive for a reason, and we ought to enjoy every minute. Maybe there should be more baby-holding time and more tea parties in our toy kitchens. Maybe there should be more back yards full of bouncy balls and hidden candy suckers. Maybe we should hug a little longer and hold on a little tighter.

Today will turn into yesterday, and today will quickly become part of the olden days. We have a to-do list that involves a lot of living and more giving than we could ever imagine.

It seems that life offers all kinds of treasure hunts, and we get to decide which to continue and which no longer make much sense to us.

Most important are the treasures we may not realize we've already sent ahead: The love and laughter we've shared with others. The cash prizes we've given to someone else. The times we've bent over backwards to lend a helping hand. The wisdom we've shared. The cares we've kept. The scars we've collected, and the tears we've helped wipe away.

Sometimes we are alone with only One witness. Sometimes not. Easy peasy.

Thank You

It was a sunny Saturday morning in November when I visited my friend Dianne. Before heading out the door, I printed out a few of my poems and stories to give to her.

The local flower shop is between her house and mine, so I stopped to choose a gift for her. I arrived at her house with a homemade chef salad, some reading material, and a white rose – just because.

After we'd visited and I was driving home, I heard a ping from my phone letting me know there was a text message. Dianne had written a note without delay. She'd read the stories I'd left with her and told me *A Groom's Prayer* had brought tears to her eyes.

I had told her I'd written it in the middle of the night when the words came to me, and someday I'd write *A Bride's Prayer*.

The next day was Thanksgiving, and my family gathered for lunch with friends. I sat beside Mary Lou, a ninety-five-year-old family friend who spoke with fondness of her son and his family. I watched how her grown grandsons cared for her. They helped her with the word games we played. They laughed with her as she pointed out the funniness and feebleness of old age.

More than a few times we heard Mary Lou say, "What would I do without them?" as she went on to list the many ways her family cares for her. Neither of us knew she was inspiring me to write about her love for her family.

My brother Stevie was with us that day and quickly accepted the assignment of handing out a wrapped yellow rose to each of the ladies.

Written at a sensible hour or not, our prayers of gratitude ought to find a place in black-and-white. A place where we can be reminded of the simple things that make life worth living.

When Grateful Prayers Are Prayed

Oh, how I love my son.

The first time I held his hands, as tiny as could be,
his five little fingers wrapped around one of mine
as if he knew it was me.

I may have marveled at his perfect little face
and wondered about the man he'd someday be,
but all that mattered was the little bundle
I held so close to me.

We lived our days in ordinary ways;
I taught him how to spell his name.

I felt the snowballs he shouldn't have thrown my way.
I saw him swipe a carrot so he could build a snowman.
Did he really take my good scarf outside
so many years ago?

I raised him in such simple times.

I really didn't believe the years would tick away so quickly,
but here we are – and they say I'm elderly now.

It makes me smile to think my son is an older guy,
for I know how young he really is.

The hard times made us stronger.
The lessons made us wiser.

All in all, it's been a good life.

A family to cherish.
Shared memories.
So many dreams ahead for them.

Oh, to live in their laughter.
To feel their strong arms.
To know their hearts.

To be the one who whispers prayers for them.

The love between us – crazy indeed.

Their love is like a gem
the only treasure ever needed.

How could it be?
Love is the only treasure we take with us
and the only treasure we'll leave behind.

If I left this world tomorrow
I would rest assured
they are covered in my love.

They'll see themselves as wonderful
and worthy by design.
They'll know their infinite potential.

They'll feel the joy that has always been ours.
They'll know when an angel has been nearby.

This little angel girl once belonged to Grandpa Leo and Grandma Patricia Oxender, and here she is in 2016, adorning a Christmas gift to their great-granddaughter Paisley.

An Amaryllis Kind of Grandmother

When we think about things that are good for us, many will agree that spending time with children is one of them. It doesn't take much to feel their positive energy. Children approach life with enthusiasm, and if we listen, they will suggest what we may want to do next.

For a child, a walk in the back yard isn't just a walk in the back yard. It can be an adventure. Children see insects, hummingbirds, and dragonflies and want to know more. They notice a tree toad and wonder if they are brave enough to hold it. They're the first to spot goldfish in the garden pond, swimming beneath the water lilies.

There was a day it occurred to me that our homes somehow change when we become grandparents, for there is a new little person on this earth who will start using the words "Grandma and Grandpa's house."

A house takes on new character when occupied by a grandparent, or an aunt, or an uncle – for a child sees a home through their own innocent eyes and discovers charm the adults may take for granted.

Perennial flower beds are not just places where flowers bloom every year – for the flowers now hold a special title, as they will be forever viewed as the kind of flowers our grandparents had. Or our neighbors had.

The barns at our aunts' and uncles' homes are not just any barns. They are the barns we played in. Children own those barn too, you know.

The smell of fresh dill in the air takes me back to our neighborhood where the Fritches were often seen in their back yard, donned in garden attire and knee-deep in produce. Never to be forgotten were their black-eyed Susans standing taller than our waistlines and in bloom every year.

When a child shares their take on things, we are reminded of the innocence of their newness to this earth and the language and culture they are learning. A comical comment from a child is valuable indeed – something we should write down so their words will not escape our memory.

As the years pass by, we discover how quickly we become the "older" person in the group. We soon learn that the vocabulary of younger people can be hard to keep up with. My mother was ninety years old and still using words from long ago. Her catchphrases were so innocent, and her words were causing others to smile as they knew she didn't know the modern-day meaning of the words she was choosing. Grandparents can say the funniest things.

A good place for retirees to gather for lunch and conversation is their local senior center. There they can be with people who are not so new to this earth and are equally interested in what their children and grandchildren are up to these days.

Years ago, when my mother's great-granddaughter McKenna was in elementary school, McKenna asked what the school planned to serve on Grandparents' Day when the children and grandparents would be eating lunch together. When McKenna heard sloppy joe sandwiches were on the menu, she stated it was a good thing because some of the old people do not have teeth and would appreciate the softer food.

McKenna's statement was one my mom always remembered and shared with her friends at the senior center and with others. Perhaps the humor in McKenna's thought is the underlying element of truth in her words: Grandparents get into issues that grandchildren take note of.

Children really don't need an explanation regarding

why "old people" begin to change their ways over the years and begin doing things at a slower pace, for they have eyes to see what's going on and ears to hear what grandparents say.

My grandson Toby was three years old when he and his mother Natalie were discussing a treat Toby proposed he should have:

Toby: "Pleeeaaaase, Mom. Pretty, pretty please."

Mom: "Stop asking me like that. I already told you 'no.'"

Toby: "Well, girls say it like that."

Mom: "Well, you're a boy, so don't."

Toby: "Please, Mom. Handsome, handsome please."

It's no wonder families take on a vocabulary of their own.

When I think of what kind of grandmother I will be remembered as, I already know it's going to be one of those amaryllis kind of grandmothers – a grandmother who takes pictures of her flowers and houseplants and feels she is looking out for others by sharing what's going on at the top of the amaryllis stem.

Certainly others appreciate my updates. Doesn't everyone want to know how much the stem grew in one day, how many blossoms appeared, and what color they are?

Doesn't everyone want to enter a grandmother's house and be escorted to the dining room table for an opportunity to check out the amaryllis growth?

It's as if the amaryllis knows it's a show-off, and it wants to hear about itself.

My grandchildren listen to my report, check out the blooms, and nod their heads in agreement to the beauty of this year's amaryllis.

Every day is a day that will eventually become a memory. Things like going on a treasure hunt. Climbing down a basement window well to catch a tree toad. Observing a grandfather napping in his chair. Watching a grandmother tend to her flowers. All custom-made memories.

When children grow up, they figure out where their treasures have been all along. Eating lunch with a grandparent (especially one who has no teeth) is, without a doubt, one of those moments they will look back on with fondness and realize they were living in the best of times.

The fingerprints of a child can often be found later when the sun shines through a window. Grandparents have been known to leave the little fingerprints right where they found them, for reasons they need not explain.

I wonder if my grandparents ever left my fingerprints on their windows. More important, I wonder if they knew they were leaving their own fingerprints upon the many little people whose lives they touched as they were simply living as grandparents live.

It may be possible to wipe away fingerprints from a windowpane, but it is impossible to wipe away the memories of learning and laughing when the old and the young spend time together.

Top Left: A photo of my amaryllis – taken on January 27, 2022.

Top Right: Here she is two days later on January 29 at 5 a.m.

Lower Right: …and again just seven hours later – at noon on January 29. A candy cane amaryllis.

Baby Toes

Admit it. You've done it. We've all done it. We've all had baby toes in our face. In fact, if there were a baby in front of you now, and the baby toes were exposed, you would touch those toes. And the baby talk would likely start. There is this pretend munching thing a lot of people do to baby toes, and it can be really funny. The baby loves it. We love it.

In fact, you are probably smiling right now as you think about baby toes.

No one really needs to tell us to enjoy the baby. We know the baby is going to grow quickly; the next thing we know there is a two-year-old in front of us. And the two-year-old will hand us their toy phone and tell us the call is for us.

All of us have answered the phone and engaged in the pretend conversation. We answer the phone with a cheerful, "Hello." We can hear ourselves saying, "Oh yes, we've been well. Thank you. And how about you?" We pause and act as if we are hearing someone speak to us. Then we say, "Yes, we would love to have you come over and play." We pause once more before replying, "Oh great! We'll see you when you get here."

We hang up the phone, but the next thing you know the phone rings again. We answer it, and this time we tell the two-year-old the call is for them.

Our little one grows from toddlerhood to childhood. We find ourselves teaching the child how to ride a bike or balance on walking stilts. Sometimes we're inside coloring a picture or sitting on the floor teaching them how to play card games we'd played when we were a child.

When we read a book to a child, we don't even need to try to feel the coziness as we sit closely beside each other. Somehow the coziness just happens.

I recently heard it said that if a child were to teach us how to spell "love," it wouldn't start with an "l." Children spell "love" with a "t," followed by an "i," and then comes an "m," and it ends with an "e."

I can remember when my daughters were young and a meal needed to find its way to the table. We can be exhausted and in need of a little downtime, but we know we must stop between all the housekeeping chores to answer the toy phone.

My grown daughter told me there are times she can't wait for Mom to have supper ready. Then she realizes she is the mom and needs to head to the kitchen. Reality check for new moms: From here on out, you are the mom.

Decades later when the phone rings, it can hit us hard when we realize our mom's name will never again appear on our caller ID.

When they say "love" is really spelled "t-i-m-e," I know it's true.

My cousin Marcella recently commented about my mom and dad's dining room table. If it could tell stories, we would all tune in to hear what it has to say.

My mom spent a lot of time in her kitchen – from 1947 to 2019. I would ask the dining room table how many cakes our mother baked during that seventy-two-year span. How many batches of sugar corn did our dad pop for us? Did any of Mom's meals ever turn out to be terrible? How many pots of ham and bean soup did she make? How many aprons did Mom go through, and how many cooks have been in the kitchen? The last earthly task my mother completed, at the age of ninety-two-and-a-half, was the baking of a chocolate birthday cake.

One of the smartest things our parents ever did was line us up and take pictures with our birthday cakes in front of us. There were times Mom served her cakes from a Depression glass cake stand.

"GRANDMA, YOU ALREADY AM OLD!"

She would count out the appropriate number of birthday candles and let us help insert them into her frosted cakes.

I imagine one of the first songs most of us learn is the "Happy Birthday" song. When you think about it, it's a comical moment in time that happens just once a year. Our best friends and relatives gather to sing to us. When we are a child, we aren't embarrassed at all. We sit and smile and listen to them sing. We even hear our name within the song.

After the candles are blown out and the little trail of smoke clears away, mothers everywhere let their children remove the candles from the cake. The technique used in most homes for the removal of frosting from the bottom of the candles is probably universal.

Next, someone who is deemed strong enough to scoop out the ice cream will take custom orders. They are told who wants a large scoop and who just wants a little bit on the plate that already holds a small, medium, or large piece of frosted birthday cake.

My mother saved the used birthday candles. Only when they became too short for proper placement on the next cake did she throw them away.

My birthday is in December, so some of my birthday photos were taken in front of the silver Christmas tree.

Mom was good about reminding me that December birthdays are especially fun, with a lot of extra festivities already taking place.

After my mother passed away, I started sorting through the many boxes of memorabilia she'd saved. I'd sit on the living room floor and lift each item from its box. It was great reading material. Later I would find I'd done more reading than sorting. I'd also created little piles that ended up being just more unsuccessful attempts at organizing the papers.

If someone were to ask me if I have a favorite find within my parents' estate, I'd have to tell them the baby toes photo is one of the best.

I didn't know a piece of paper could make me feel as if I were the richest person in the world. It wasn't a box of silver and gold I had been sorting through. There were no rubies or gems to unearth. I had simply opened a cardboard box and discovered a 3x3 piece of paper we call a "photo."

My dad was dressed up in the picture, so I think we were spending time together on a Sunday afternoon. Dad was lying on the floor with his feet propped up on a chair. A baby was resting in Dad's arms, and the baby's toes were clearly in the face of my brother Don.

The snapshot captured a carefree moment of a father playing with his son and baby girl.

There I was, on my own living room floor, examining a photo I had never seen before, knowing the man on the floor was my dad and the young boy was my brother Don. The photo was stamped "Aug" with no year behind it. Don appears to be about six years old in the photo, which confirmed the baby was me.

That little piece of paper made me pause and just sit still. How could there have been a photo such as this in my parents' house, and I didn't even know about it?

Then I remembered: My mom was busy raising her children, and she had a lot of toy phones to answer over the years.

Her intentions were probably to go back and organize things someday. She never got it done. That's okay; she was too busy living her life. She was a history buff. She was writing about things from long ago, and I am left finding those things from long ago.

At one time, it seemed the boxes of saved newspaper clippings, letters, schoolwork, and artwork were such a burden to us. They represented hours of work ahead, but the little treasures we are finding are treasures indeed. My siblings and cousins have had more than a few fun conversations about the memorabilia.

Our parents, aunts, and uncles are gone now, and life seems to have taken on a bit of a twist. I look at a lot of things differently as I remember more of the good times than the bad.

After I began sorting through my parents' estate, it was fun telling friends I had started writing about the items in my parents' home.

I remember telling them about finding a photo and writing a story about baby toes. Of course I thought the story ended there. I didn't know there was a magazine that'd been published in 1962 waiting for me to find in one of the boxes of memorabilia.

I was at my parents' house one morning before my brother Stevie would be leaving for his workday. The two of us had been rushed because both of us had overslept. It was a scramble to get his scrambled eggs made and to see him out the front door.

I decided to relax for a few minutes before cleaning his kitchen and heading home, so I went to the nearest box of my mother's memorabilia and found an old magazine. The cover was pink, and it was entitled "Congratulations." The baby on the front of the magazine happened to be a baby playing with her toes.

I settled into a reclining chair and thought, *The only thing I'm going to read from this publication is information directed at parents way back whenever this magazine had been put together.*

On the first page of the magazine was a hospital birth record completed with an ink pen and cursive handwriting. And there was my name. It was certainly another heartwarming moment, but my thoughts were, *Oh no. Here we go again. This is about me.*

Apparently, a hospital employee had written some of the information using black ink. On the top line of this official Hospital Birth Record was my first name, penned in black ink. My middle and last name were written by my mother in blue ink.

The second line tells us the baby was born to Mr. and Mrs. Vernon Kimpel. Next came the time of my birth: 3:08 in the afternoon. I never knew that.

My date of birth, followed by the name of the hospital and the city and state, were filled in. Dr. Boerger and the hospital administrator's signatures were at the bottom.

It looked so official, yet the last paragraph simply made me smile. The page was supposed to have an "Official Seal" affixed to it, but the seal had never been applied to this hospital birth record. Oh well.

I turned the page to discover the back side of the certificate had been stamped with baby toes. I needed a moment. Those footprints were apparently mine. And my mother had left her thumbprint. So had Dad. There I sat – staring at my parents' thumbprints.

I wondered if they'd conspired to play a joke on me. My dad could have said, "Hey, let's take this baby magazine home, hide it in a box of stuff, and let her find it someday."

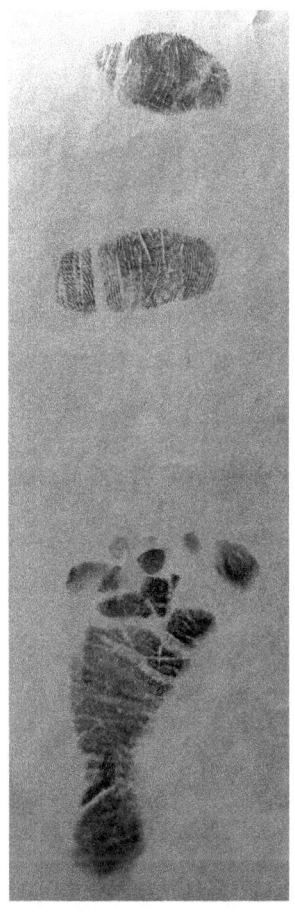

I didn't know what to think. I'd been writing about baby toes and thought the story was over. But there I was – staring at a clear image of my own baby toes that'd been stamped in a baby magazine at the time of my birth.

I imagine my dad was visiting Mom in the hospital, and a nurse who was in charge of the fingerprinting made sure the task was completed. Thank goodness someone had an important job that day. Those who were present would never know the footprints were going into a time capsule for the baby girl to find more than half a century later.

With tears in my eyes, I slowly read the rest of the magazine. I found some interesting ads for canned milk, liquid baby aspirin, and articles that were intended to educate parents on current trends.

Mom recorded my birth weight in the magazine: 7 pounds, 2 ¾ ounces. She had documented the name of the attending nurse: M Coy, R.N. And my grandparents' names are on the family tree.

Of course I thought I could finish my baby toes story after writing about the magazine, but then I spent a Sunday evening with my brothers Stevie and Ed and my sister-in-law Sue.

Stevie joined in the conversation that night, and as Stevie often did, he started his crazy laughter. It seemed everything was funnier than it should have been, and he was making the rest of us laugh.

He laughed at the baby toes photo and asked if the baby was himself. He asked what year the photo was taken and told us that he wasn't even born yet. I expanded the picture on my phone, and he could see the baby toes were in his brother Don's face.

Stevie knew why the baby toes were in Don's face, but that didn't stop him from asking about it. I reminded Stevie that if he had some baby toes in front of himself right now, he too would be playing with them. He laughed in agreement and did an impersonation of how people play with baby toes. He even blew on the imaginary toes and cracked himself up.

Sue caught Stevie's laughter on her phone camera and forwarded the video to our siblings. We decided Stevie had probably enjoyed more than a half-hour's worth of laughter before he headed to bed. As he was falling asleep, I heard him speaking out loud about baby toes. He chuckled as he fell asleep.

Whoever grabbed my father's camera back in the summer of 1963 obviously knew they were capturing a playful moment. What they didn't know was how many years would pass before the family would find the photo stored in a cardboard box and tucked away in a closet.

As I was typing my baby toes story, I remembered there was a black-and-white photo of me in front of the silver Christmas tree with a toy phone in my hand. I was willing to guess I was two years old when the picture was taken. I started the search for that snapshot and found it in the second shoebox I'd sorted through. I was, indeed, two years old when the picture was taken.

I wonder how many bicycles my dad had put together and how many wooden toys he'd made for his children to find under the tree on Christmas morning. Mom certainly spent more time wrapping presents than it took for her children to unwrap them.

My mother is no longer here to call me on my birthday each December. My parents are not here to give me a gift, yet here I am still opening gifts they left behind. They also left me with a fun younger brother to take care of. It seems that all a parent could give a daughter, they did.

A photo of me on December 16, 1964, taken in front of our silver Christmas tree.

A Baby Joes Prayer

It was after my mother passed away when I found a box of greeting cards that'd been sent to my family at the time of my birth in December of 1962. Some of my baby cards were holiday cards.

I didn't know this box of memorabilia even existed. But there it was – along with many other boxes – waiting for me to find it. Mom had even saved some of the wrapping paper from the gifts she'd received.

My Aunt Joan wrote that she was out of baby cards, so she was sending a letter. In 1962, my Aunt Joan and Uncle Clair were the parents of four boys: Kim, Jim, Neal, and Jeff.

I was born a week before Christmas. On a Sunday. According to Aunt Joan's letter, they had planned to visit my family that day, but Mom was in the hospital. Aunt Joan wrote, "You changed our plans, it's all over now and you have your girl. But how did you get a girl?"

She went on to write, "They all love and kiss Jeff so much and it makes him mad." And later in the letter, "Jeff spits and sputters and all the boys can do is laugh at him, then he thinks he's cute and does more."

According to Aunt Joan, Jimmy had said he wouldn't give Jeff up, but he'd "take a baby girl too."

Little did the family know, a couple of years later, the four boys would receive their little sister. And they named her Beth Ann. It may be safe to say Beth Ann was okay with all the kisses from her four older brothers.

One of my baby cards was from our neighbor, Mrs. Hug. We never called her by her first name. The neighborhood children have always known her as "Mrs. Hug."

It's a heartwarming thought – our neighbor lady's name was Mrs. Hug. Her last name fit her personality. She wore an apron over her dress. Her voice was soft and sweet. She made sugar cookies with gumdrops in them. She kept cookies in the cookie jar on her kitchen table. She made lye soap, and I still love the smell and feel of a bar of lye soap.

Everyone should grow up with a Mrs. Hug in their life.

Mrs. Hug had written this note on the back of the baby card she'd sent to my parents: "I was so glad when the girls came over and told me about their little sister but I guess I wasn't the only one they were really tickled about it just what they wanted a baby girl. Marlene will be thrilled when she finds out that you named it after her. I told the girls when they came over and told me about it that will make a nice Christmas present and they said that's what Marcia said when she was putting up the tree. You will be home now for Christmas you knew just when to go you had that arranged purty nice. I hope everything goes well with you and the baby take good care of yourself. Mrs. Flora Hug."

My mom would have arrived home, with baby number nine, just a few days before Christmas. Like all families, the older children helped care for their younger siblings.

When we see a new baby, we often see perfection. We

see beauty in their eyes and life in their smile. We plan for wonderful days ahead. It's a time in our lives when grateful prayers are prayed.

A Baby Toes Prayer

Dear Lord, we love You
and we love our sweet baby, so perfect and new.

We are in awe of his tiny frame.

We love him from the top of his beautiful head
to the tips of his little baby toes.

You have placed him in our tender care,
and we pray to enjoy every day of his life.

We pray for gentle wisdom and Your voice to hear
as we nurture him and watch him grow up so fast.

Please bless him with wonderful play, a love for life,
and protection while he sleeps.

As he grows up big and strong,
we pray his love for You grows big,
and his calling grows bold.

You will hear the first prayer our baby whispers,
and every prayer and promise that follows.
We pray for Your mighty hand upon his life.

We ask You to bless his future with
laughter and innocent mischief
as he enjoys many
cherished and lasting friendships.

Lord, we are always children in Your eyes.
You were with us when we drew the breath of life,
and You are with us as we grow old.

May our beautiful baby someday find in his heart
many memories of a wonderful life he lived for You,

And we thank You for his beautiful baby toes.

"GRANDMA, YOU ALREADY AM OLD!"

Being a Grandmother

I have learned to enjoy where I am
on the way to where I will someday be.

Bedtime stories
I've read aplenty.

That little bit of dust, I simply looked away.
Cobwebs were told to quiet down.
I was rocking my baby,
and babies don't keep.

Fingerprints on my window:
I shall not wipe away
for their little hands left evidence
I spent time with a child the other day.

Hugs may have been around my shoulders
and kisses were on my lips,
but they've settled in my heart –
a heart condition indeed.

My children knew how to dig in dirt
and catch all kinds of creatures.

They were watchful 'round flowerpots –
for little tree toads were waiting to jump out!

Put your arms around me once again if you really care
for your love is the only way to protect me
from the invisible bugs you think are there.

I learned when I was just a girl –
"germ" means "life."

Let's plant some seeds in dirt
and watch them germinate!
Grandma knows what invisible bugs
are capable of.

Bossing germs around?
There's no need.
The universe knows what it's doing.

The glow of candles on birthday cakes
one candle for each year.

We'll sing a song of birthday wishes
and include your name, so dear.

A healthy burst of air will put those candles out.

The icing on the cake
baptized indeed with germs!

Now the strongest arm is usually in charge
of the silver scoop and ice cream.

There's chocolate fudge to drizzle
and sprinkles to be sprinkled.
And who will place the cherries on top?

With hands in the air
the kids we can hear
a cheerful, "Pick me!"

They'll watch and make sure
y'all get a share
as desserts are divvied up.

We need not wait for a special occasion
to live each spectacular moment.

To live a good life.
Grand at times.
Away from the noise of the world.

"GRANDMA, YOU ALREADY AM OLD!"

I'm the old one now.

Sunsets
I've seen many.

Ballgames
I've cheered on.

Hugs
they've been aplenty.

Goodbyes
with tiny tears in our eyes.

The day will come
when I say my last goodbye.

Listen closely to my whisper
right on cue – I'll tell you I love you.

So let's get together while we can.
Bring your smiles and your laughter
and pretty flowers in your hand.
Pick some green beans from the garden.
We'll sit on the porch
and let everyone help snip them.

You make such a difference
when you call or you visit.

Tell Grandma she is loved
and be generous with your kisses!

If she bakes you a cake
a large helping you must take.

If she stirs up some beverage,
it's the best flavor ever!

She knows what to do
with the bugs you have left her;
she appreciates your hugs
as well as those bugs.

Someday the grandchildren will reminisce.

What will they say?
she wonders.

Will it be the gardens and flower beds
or the smell of food in the air?

Will it be the tickles
or the popcorn
or the crazy writing of stories?

One thing she hopes
her grandchildren will see:

Grandma's loving where she is
on the way to where she will someday be.

This Year's Model

Oh, the things I've learned from items made of paper. If it weren't for the reading material my mother left behind, I would never have known so many interesting details about the long-standing friendship between my family and the Jennings family. My mother's friends, two sisters by the last name of Jennings, married two brothers by the last name of Sanders.

I've found photos from their high school days and their weddings. Paper invitations to showers and parties. Letters and greeting cards. Little notes that give us a hint of what life was like for them as they were raising their families. The newspaper clippings let us know who were the hosts and who were the guests at their many gatherings.

Maxine Jennings grew up and married John Sanders. The two were classmates and graduated together from Edgerton High School in 1942. I have a copy of the 1977 *Edgerton Earth* newspaper in which the town's homecoming events and class reunion photos were featured. A photo of Maxine, John, and their classmates, who were gathering for their 35th class reunion, can be found in that paper.

Maxine's younger sister, Margaret, married John's older brother, Roy. The children of siblings who marry are called "double cousins."

My parents and their friends were known to have potlucks at each other's homes. Surprise potlucks to boot. Now that is something I could get used to. How about I look out my window at suppertime and find four or five cars in my driveway? And my best friends carrying food into my home. They smile as they hold open the door for each other.

Even if my house were a little on the messy side when they show up with supper in hand, I would quickly make room and grab extra chairs – anything to make them feel at home.

When we find a photo of ourselves gathered with friends, we are reminded of days gone by. It is not unusual to hear the words "Look at how young we were. And how thin."

Age is a funny thing. We've never been this old before, yet we are as young today as we are ever going to be.

How easily we may forget that every grandmother and every grandfather was once the mom or the dad. As I sort through the memorabilia my mother left behind, I marvel at their lifestyle. The "How did they do it?" thoughts never end.

There was no date on a baby card Maxine had sent to my mother, but a little detective work tells us she mailed the card after my sister Jayne was born in October of 1951.

Maxine wrote: "Dear Ruth, Can't keep up with my supply of baby cards so will have to substitute. You did right well in 'picking' a date for your daughter to be born. Johnny and I were just talking about it being unusual for us to be your attendants for your wedding, and then for you to have a boy on Johnny's birthday and a girl on mine. They can't help but be wonderful kids!! A week ago or so I told Johnny I just bet you'd have this one on my birthday but could hardly believe it when I heard it happened. Each one is just as nice and wonderful as the first one. They aren't as much trouble as I thought they might be. We'll try to stop in to see the latest model. Best wishes to you and yours. Sincerely, Maxine."

My brother Ed was born on October 8th which was Johnny's 25th birthday, and my sister Jayne was born on October 24th which was Maxine's 27th birthday.

In a large family, the birth order is a fun thing to follow. My parents' firstborn was Marcia. Then a son, Ed, followed by three girls – Jayne, Elaine, and Carolyn. When my brother Don was born, Maxine wrote "Was real glad for you (and Eddie) that you got your boy!"

Her letter also included a paragraph with her thoughts about her family at the time. "I used to think that six kids was more than I'd want to handle but I guess you never hear a mother complain that she has too many. After they are here there just doesn't seem to be a one you could get along without."

After the arrival of my brother Don came Darrell, and then Lee, so three boys in a row worked out when it came to playing ball and growing up together.

One of Maxine's letters that was especially interesting is one in which she starts with a welcome to the '59 model. This means her words were written in September after Darrell was born. She wrote: "Things have slowed down around here to a fast walk. I'm so far behind in ironing, when I open the washroom door, baskets of clothes to be ironed fall out like it were Fibber McGee's closet."

Maxine's referral to Fibber McGee made me look up who Fibber was as well as ask my older friends if they remembered Fibber McGee. The online short videos of Fibber are humorous and explain why the closet was noteworthy.

Maxine also wrote about the garden food she'd canned that summer. She was canning her last batch of ketchup and then quitting except for apples. She had already completed ninety-some quarts each of peaches, tomatoes, string beans, and corn. Then odd amounts of strawberries, lima beans, and red kidney beans.

She also wrote their "garden was somewhat of a fizzle because of dry weather. Cabbage, celery, Chinese cabbage were a complete flop."

Her next paragraph tells us that she was watching Doug (Roy and Margaret's baby) that day. She needed to finish the ketchup, make potato salad, bake two pies, frost a layer cake, and have everyone ready to go to a wiener roast at five for Mary Lu's birthday. In-between she needed to iron a basket of dampened clothes. That evening at 8:30 she was going to a church meeting. And there she was, writing a letter to my mom when she needed to get busy with one of the most magnificent to-do lists I've ever read.

The words "How did she do it?" come to mind every time I read her note.

When I met with Maxine to tell her about her letters and the photos I'd found in my parents' estate, I asked her about a church meeting that started at 8:30 p.m. She told me that meetings and gatherings indeed started late in the evenings, for people were busy working all day but could meet at a late hour. Maxine kindly identified people in unlabeled photographs from my mother's collection of old black-and-whites.

When I was born in December of 1962, I was the ninth

child brought into a home where I'd grow up with four older sisters and four older brothers. I imagine they were happy when it was their turn to hold the new baby.

Three years later Jeanette was born, and the two of us became the little blond girls in the family. Steven was the eleventh child and loved being the baby of the family.

I discovered in Mom's notes that Maxine and John's nine children were always born near the time each of the Kimpel children were born. I am told there was a joke that my mom didn't get the memo that it was okay to stop after nine children. Mom went on to have Jeanette and Steven.

Maxine and John's eldest child, Ruthie, was named after my mother. Ruthie's circle of friends included my oldest sister Marcia. My oldest brother Ed remembers playing at the Sanders' home with Jim Sanders, while my sister Jayne was friends with Judy Sanders. Then an interesting turn of events happened when the Sanders family welcomed two boys, Dave and Bob, at the time the Kimpels brought home two girls, Elaine and Carolyn.

It really was true that my mother and Maxine were having babies at the same time. The Sanders went on to have three girls – Becky, Anita, and Pat, while the Kimpels were busy with three boys – Don, Darrell, and Lee.

In my baby card, which was a holiday card, Maxine penned "Congratulations on your new daughter. Wish I could trade places with you and have mine done. Only we ordered the male model. But John says 'he' is a girl!" She signed the card "Maxine, Johnny, and family."

For the record, the Sanders family found out John's prediction was incorrect. Their ninth baby, Keith, was indeed the male model they had placed an order for.

In the mix of children who grew up together were those who belonged to Roy and Margaret Sanders – Mike, Marty, Rita, and Doug. And the Jennings cousins – Greg, Steve, Gary, Kay, Mark, Jeff, and Holly – the children of Kenneth and Phyllis Jennings.

By the time the 1970s rolled around, the oldest children had begun graduating from high school. Some were in college or had joined the military.

According to one of Mom's newspaper clippings, on October 31 of 1970, one of the Jennings grandchildren decided to be born that day – at home.

The story goes that Maxine and Margaret's nephew, Greg Jennings, called his mother-in-law, Marge Lemke, to advise her that his wife, Janet, was going to be having the baby soon. Marge was to drive fast, go to the church kitchen, and pick up Greg's mother, Phyllis Jennings, who was a nurse. Who better to deliver a baby at home than your mother who is a nurse. I can just imagine one grandmother racing into the church basement telling the other grandmother that she needed to run quick. The two ladies would have been in their forties at the time, so "running quick" was not a problem.

The article states that when the two grandmothers arrived at the Jennings' home, the father-to-be was yelling: "What took you so long?"

It was a Saturday morning, and Phyllis probably thought the only excitement she was going to have that day would be helping Maxine and Margaret in the church kitchen. The ladies needed to make one hundred dozen doughnuts for the Halloween party at St. Francis College in Fort Wayne. But by the end of the day, Phyllis was able to say she'd delivered her first baby who happened to be her first grandchild, she called the doctor to report the news, and she helped make one hundred dozen doughnuts.

The newspaper article tells us that Krill's ambulance drove mother and baby girl, Amy, to DeKalb Memorial Hospital in Auburn, Indiana.

And so it would be – the next generation would begin the start of the 1970 models.

I was left wondering about the doughnuts. What was their recipe? Did their children help with the making of the one hundred dozen doughnuts? Did they frost the doughnuts or dip them in cinnamon and sugar? Certainly they made extras to take home. And those who were involved in the delivery of the baby sat down for a doughnut break. Can you imagine the fun conversation the church basement ladies were engaged in after learning about the arrival of this new little model?

With each morning sunrise, we know not where the day will take us. No one could have imagined the delivery of a first grandchild was on a grandmother's to-do list. Phyllis thought the only reason she was driving to town was to help her sisters-in-law. But part of the beauty of life is in the surprise.

At the end of each day, we can be grateful for the things in our life that force us to take a moment to be in the moment. Even if the moment requires our legs to run fast.

Every day is full of invitations to let the day be more beautiful than we could imagine. Life doesn't always go as planned, and that's a good thing. If we were to get everything we wanted, we would be limiting ourselves to the possibilities of greater things than we could ever dream of on our own.

"GRANDMA, YOU ALREADY AM OLD!"

A photo of some of the memorabilia my mother had saved.
Below the picture of the Jennings family are the words:
SOMEWHAT UNUSUAL CIRCUMSTANCES
surrounded this five-generation get-together Monday night.
Introductions were in order all around for week-old
Amy Jennings in the arms
of her great-great-grandparents, Mr. and Mrs. Harry Souder, seated,
while in back (Left to right) are father Greg Jennings,
grandmother, Mrs. Phyllis Jennings,
and great grandfather Ralph Souder. The Souders are from Butler.
The youngster was in an awful hurry to get here
and meet all her new relatives.
The first child of the local Jennings', she was born in their N. Michigan St. home about an hour after her mother's first warning labor pains.

The Grandmother in My Mirror

Those who've sorted through an estate have likely found a photo or two in which no one knows who's in the picture. The snapshots with a cake in the center are the best. If we don't know the story, we look for someone who does. In many families, the oldest siblings and cousins are asked if they know anything about the day the photo was taken.

With each passing year, there are jokes about how many candles it would take to properly decorate our birthday cake. Birthday candles are available in twenty-four packs. How quickly we move into the three-pack category.

Young people are graduating during the month of May, and they've already been told how quickly the years are going to zoom by.

It seems we're all the same. We think a thirty-year-old is "old." Somewhere in our twenties, we decide thirty isn't old. And so it goes with each passing decade.

One thing we can agree upon is the fact that we change – emotionally, mentally, and physically. We're the same person we've always been, yet we are not.

The day comes when we look in the mirror and see the reflection of a grandparent staring back at us. We wonder how it was we thought grandparents were old. How wonderful it is to discover that we're not old – we just look that way.

The Grandmother in My Mirror

Can anybody tell me, where did the little girl go?
I used to see her looking back at me
when she peered into the mirror,
but apparently she went somewhere.
Can I report her as missing?

The little girl had shiny blonde hair,
big brown eyes, and long eyelashes.
She loved to wear dresses and carry little purses.
She really did sell poppies
when she was just a young girl.

I know it's true: She grew up.
She moved away and got married.
She had children.
Then her children did the same.

That's when the grandmother showed up in her mirror.
I told her she doesn't have to look
and act so much like a grandmother,
but she doesn't listen.

Her hair went from blonde to salt-and-pepper grey
and sometimes I see a glisten.

Her face used to be that of a young lady,
but she's starting to look like her mother!

You ought to hear her talk.
Those words of hers –
proof she thinks just like a grandmother.

And that guy who lived in her house – he's gone too.

There's a grandfather walking around here.
He used to talk of fishing trips
and the wonder of the great outdoors.
Now he speaks of grandchildren.
He's buying fishing poles, baseball bats, and more.

The grandma and grandpa seem to understand
they are still young.

They know someday the young grandparents
will move out, and the old ones will move in,

Once again they'll want to make a report
about whom they think is missing.

Is there a way a mirror can help them out
as they become old grandparents?

There are lotions and tweezers galore around here,
yet nothing seems to work.

I need to let them know they are as young today as ever.
Tomorrow they'll be another day older.

It seems their birthdays roll around so quickly each year.

Their family and friends walk right in,
arms full of boxes with pretty bows on top.

Bouquets of flowers and balloons galore
now part of their home's décor.

Birthday cards aplenty in the porch mailbox.

The candles on the cake – now there by the dozens.

But no need to fear, the firemen are aware of the hazards
of so many candles aflame.

With sirens in the air and fire hoses in strong hands
they kindly show up at a moment's notice.

They'll extinguish the flames,
then wish you another good year.
Thank heavens they do their work with such cheer.

No need to report anyone as missing.
It finally happened –
the young grandparents moved out
and the old moved in.

The grandmother now peeks into her mirror
and sees it quite clear –
there's a great-grandmother living
on the outside of her.

When Grandma's friends come to visit,
they laugh and reminisce.
Listen closely and you will hear
the voice of the little girl still inside of her.

Birthday parties were fun when she was a kid.
But as the years passed by,

speaking of her birthday
was met with a ladylike hush.

Then Grandma got older and thought it all over.
Perhaps those who love her
really do know best?

The birthday celebrations started up again
very big and oh, so grand!

But everyone's learned their lesson
and the firemen were put on notice:

Grandma is adding another candle this year!

Dear Younger Me

I imagine many of us have dreamt of going back in time and having a talk with the younger version of ourself. As we grow older, we have gained worldly wisdom we could offer to youngsters. We can offer, but who's listening?

Someone asked me if the thirty-year-old me would have listened to a sixty-year-old me. I would like to think so. I know the sixty-year-old me would listen to a ninety-year-old me, because I already listen to those who are older than I.

A ninety-year-old version of me would definitely see me as a youngster. She would tell me to relish the fact I can put on a coat, search for my missing car keys yet again, and scurry out the door because I'm running a few minutes late.

She would tell me to appreciate being the young one in

the group of ladies. The one who can drive in the dark or in the rain. The one who drops off the others at the door.

The older me would tell me that I still have plenty of time to make mistakes. I will flub up. My friends will flub up. We don't have to talk about it. If it's laughable – then laugh. If it's fixable – then fix it. If it's workable – then work on it.

I would be told to remember that "cherish" is my favorite word. She would remind me to take care of myself. And care for those around me – for caring about others is one of a few fun ways to collect treasures.

She would tell me that old age is a time when we realize we have spent too many hours focused on what doesn't matter. But even that doesn't matter. We have lived. We have learned. We have loved.

Would the older me point out the fact I will never again be the me I am right now? Should I slow down and spend some time with the current me?

I once heard it said that we turn not older with years, but newer every day. And now I get it: We are a newer version of our self with each passing day.

Every evening, we can recognize the ordinary and not-so-ordinary things that happened during the day. It seems we never stop learning. We never stop growing. We know we have things to teach and share with those who are younger.

As babies, we are born with beautiful baby toes, just as they were meant to be. As we enter into old age, our feet sometimes ache, are a bit worn out, and are not nearly as cute as they used to be.

Perhaps it is during our quiet time when we are reminded of the masterpiece we are – from the start of our life right through to the end. We don't have to be more, yet sometimes we are. We don't have to do more, yet sometimes we do.

When we are gentle with ourselves and listen to those who have some wisdom to share, perhaps we would choose to slow down. Perhaps we would learn to appreciate the newest version of the youngest person we will ever be: The me I am today.

A photo taken on the day of my sister Marcia's college graduation reception in 1970.
From left to right: Jeanette, Marcia, and Marlene.

Country Roads

What do you do when your friend calls you on a Monday morning to tell you how her weekend went? You listen.

If you're a writer, you know when "there's a story there." The person on the other end of the phone doesn't know you're jotting down their words.

My friend Elaine had decided to take the scenic route on her way to a Sunday morning church service and ended up with a story to tell about her trek on back country roads.

It's only later, when you recognize yourself as a character in a story, that you remember your friend is a writer. And anything you say or do can be used in a story.

Grandma Is Lost!

It's Sunday morning.
Where could she be?

The service will soon be starting.
Look out the window and pray!

Everyone's worried and very concerned.
Is she here yet?

Why is she not answering her flip phone?

Grandma, we're getting nervous.
Your grandson will soon be standing in the pulpit!

His first sermon ever – please hurry and get here!

No sign of her yet in the church parking lot?
Oh where could our grandmother be?

Quick! Someone call her neighbor
who'll make sure she's okay.

The neighbor's so helpful with a quick response:
Grandma and her car are nowhere to be found!
Where in the world could she be?

Whom should we call next?
If anyone would know, it would be the State Patrol!

They kindly report no recent accidents.
They too are concerned –
where could your grandmother be?

She's 87 years old and has no GPS!

It's Grandma who knows why she's running late –
she simply turned right when it should have been a left.

No worries,
in just a few minutes she'll arrive at the church.
She'll smile and let them know
she was simply enjoying the scenic route.

She turned once again and made it worse.
If another turn is needed – should it be north?
Or could it be south?

Certainly she'll find someone who'll know –
just look for the person out taking a stroll.

She drives and she watches.
Why in the world is no one around?

Just pull in the drive of a nice-looking house.
A knock upon the door will surely suffice.
The people inside will be ever so happy
to help a little white-haired lady.
The cane in her hand will give them a clue
they should answer the door
and tell her what to do.

Oh where could that church be?
The one with the tall steeple!

No one is home
not even at the next house!

There's a barn door wide open
but no farmer to be found.

Why, oh why, are there no people around?

Grandma has plenty of fuel in her car.
She looks at her watch – it's time that's running out!

She's back on the road
and the prayers are flyin':

I believe it's time for
Someone Else to take hold of the wheel.

The family decides they must find her
and head out the door to the church parking lot.

Abruptly the keys find a place in the ignition.
The tires move forward in tandem.
The steering wheel's aware of the tight turns it's making.

Astonished, the motor obeys as it's told to gear up.
The dashboard is ready for extravagant numbers!

Oh what a relief when her car passes by.
Mission accomplished –
we found our sweet grandma!

A simple text message will calm all the worries.
We'll let them know her car just passed by us!

The message is sent that Grandma just passed –
but gone were the words "by us."

The excitement of the moment could easily be blamed.
The grandson now reads his text message:
"Grandma has passed."

Of course, his heart sinks.
He must pull himself together and do so quite fast.

He walks to the lobby and whom does he see?
It's Grandma! Wonderfully alive and up on two feet!

Oh, why did he read a text message so shocking
when clearly we see
our grandmother is walking and talking!

She smiles as she's helped to the sanctuary pew –
It's her grandson's sermon she gets to listen to!

She settles in her seat and can't help but notice
how enthralled they all are by the words being spoken!

Now the service is over and we head out the door.
No worries 'bout roadblocks or any detours:

It's just life that takes us where we never thought we'd go.

We gather for lunch and spend time together.
Grandma is delighted to offer the prayer.
With heads gently bowed and hands softly folded
we hear her sweet voice and her kind, gentle prayer.

She gives thanks for her family
and the food that's before us.
Oh my, how the great-grandchildren are growing!

Her path has been lit and she's ever so thankful:
a reminder we need never feel lost.

Grandma ends her prayer in traditional fashion
then shares thoughts from her grandmotherly heart –

Who'd have imagined there'd someday be
a phone that knows how to get you
where you'd like to be?

Thank goodness you young ones
know the latest in technology.

With the greatest of ease and ever so kindly –
you're ready and willing with the best of directions.
Keeping us old folks in line.

Grandma, in turn, has some wisdom to share.
She speaks of a kind gentle Voice
deep down in our hearts.

With the greatest of ease and ever so kindly –
It's ready and willing with the best of directions.

And all you have to do, dear ones, is listen!

A photo from my mother's collection of newspaper clippings.

So What's Your Superpower?

My grandchildren were together recently playing in our living room, and I was watching their antics. Adults can easily forget that we, too, once darted from the couch to wherever we wanted to be in a few short seconds.

There was a day when all of us joined in somersault races across the living room floor. Little bodies are so capable of doing whatever they need to do. There is no slowness or stiffness when we are a child.

The four little cousins were playing hard while discussing their superpowers, and they seemed to know what their individual powers were.

One of them asked what my superpower was. They stopped their jumping and playing and looked at me. Rather blank looks. They were waiting for Grandma's answer.

The question seemed to loom in the air: Could a grandparent have a superpower? Especially grandmothers?

I thought it would take a while to come up with an answer. My first thought was I am good at tickling. After all, there is an art to the tickle, and a little girl from a big family would know that.

But I passed on giving them the tickle answer and moved on to the real answer.

I told them I have a superpower over four people in my life. When I haven't seen them in a while, I notice they run to me. They hug me. They can't resist their grandmother. They smile. I feel the spirit of a superpower within me.

Then they move on to their grandfather who has the same power. His Grandpa Superpower is probably mightier than the Grandma Superpower. And that's okay. There is something about grandfathers with their grandchildren.

So they listened to my answer and realized my superpower had something to do with them, and thus they have power over me.

They could choose to withhold their love from their grandparents. They could choose to be stingy with their hugs and kisses. They have the power to stop my superpower, and they told me that. They laughed as they suggested they will not be controlled any longer.

But it's not a laughing matter when people who are close to each other decide to not love each other. Marriage problems may start, and spouses begin to take each other for granted. Those who withhold love from the one they once held dear obviously don't realize they have stripped their loved one of their superpower.

The day will likely arrive when they know where that pain in their foot is coming from. When you shoot yourself in the foot, it hurts.

Can loving each other be maintained when only one person is towing the line? On the other hand, our superpowers are put to good use when we love the way others love us. And the way we love them back. When we are happy to see them and want to spend time with them.

Today's grandchildren know what it's like to see their phone contacts appear on the screen. If the screen lights up with "Grandma" or "Grandpa," they may know to cherish the time they are still in connection with a grandparent.

There will be a day when Grandma and Grandpa's names will no longer appear on their caller ID. Gone is their wisdom. Gone are their superpowers over them. Gone is their opportunity to pick up the phone and say, "Hey, what you doing?"

I decided to write about the day I had spoken with my grandchildren about their superpowers. I called Thomas so he could remind me what his superpower is. He said that is easy: "Speed." He even spelled it for me and explained he is a superfast kid. Faster than his mother. Definitely faster than his grandmother.

Thomas and I talked about how a grandparents' superpower over their grandchildren seems to work if a grandchild's heart allows it. He thinks kids should always make sure the grandmothers and grandfathers in this world keep their power.

Then Deano got on the phone, and he said that he can get a hold of anyone's cheeks and make them look chubby. I told him that is quite the superpower.

I called Paisley, who said that she can turn into an animal. I asked her how, and she said she just imagines she is an animal. She is very often an eagle, and she can fly. She agreed it is fun to be able to fly.

My oldest grandson Toby said he has lots of imagined superpowers, but he knows he is good at using drumsticks to make neat sounds come off a drum.

I told Toby about my superpower over my four grandchildren, and he agreed grandchildren should always help grandparents maintain their superpower.

Toby asked what Grandpa's power would be, and we decided Grandpa can take pieces of wood into his workshop and make the wood look like a piece of furniture or a beautiful ornament. Grandpa can make fish bite. He can make logs burn when he builds his campfires. He can make sugar corn in a kettle on the stovetop. It seems Grandpa Oxender has many superpowers.

Toby and I laughed at Deano's ability to make someone else's cheeks look chubby, and the two of us agreed it was one of the best superpowers there ever could be.

The Superpower Disclaimer:

Never let your superpowers fade away. As you grow older, the grandchildren will visit. They will expect a batch of sugar corn, and you'd better remember how to get it done. They might want to build a campfire or see how the fish are biting in the lakes nearby.

The children in our lives will come to realize a beautiful life doesn't just happen. There are talents to nurture. Things to learn. Fun times to be scheduled.

We grandparents may no longer be able to join in the somersault races, and we may lose out on any superpower that involves speed, but the Chubby Cheek Superpower, we can do that.

A photo of our grandchildren Toby, Deano, Paisley, and Thomas showing how the Chubby Cheek Superpower works.

Over-the-Top

It was in the spring of 2017 when the Watoto Children's Choir from Africa was scheduled for a performance in our hometown of Montpelier, Ohio.

The members of the choir would be traveling by bus and arriving in the middle of a weekday afternoon. They'd perform an evening show on stage at the church and stay overnight before heading out on their tour bus to travel to their next destination.

If we could help out by providing sleeping accommodations for them, we were to let the church office know.

I hesitated to volunteer because our upstairs bedrooms had taken on the role of storage rooms. The cleaning of the spare bedrooms had stayed perpetually on my to-do list. So I was thinking of myself when I signed up to be a host family. I would have a reason to focus on the cleaning of the upstairs bedrooms.

The choir members travel by bus across the United States from one destination to the next. Ten adults and twenty children. I remember thinking about the chaperones who travel for six months. With twenty children. In a bus. I couldn't see myself in a job such as that.

The group had started their six-month tour in Texas. Their destinations were booked so they would be traveling north in hopes of experiencing mild weather as they reached each new location.

On the day of the performance, my Aunt Isabel happened to stop by my house. I told her I was doing some last-minute cleaning before some little girls would be staying with us. Isabel was interested in attending the show, so she went home and recruited a couple of her teenage great-grandsons to attend with her.

Of course it ended up being an enjoyable evening, and their stage performance was inspiring.

As impressed as I was with their ability to sing and dance, I was soon going to learn the most inspiring part of my experience would be the incredible politeness shown by the children.

Their manners were apparent right away. They knew how to introduce themselves, and they learned our names. In their culture, the adults are referred to as "Auntie" and "Uncle." So we were immediately "Auntie Marlene" and "Uncle Pat."

The three children who would be staying with us were

Scarlet, Bella, and Daphne. Auntie Gloria was their chaperone. Gloria was a young woman with a beautiful voice, and she was a soloist.

After the show, the girls knew the drill. Their backpacks were placed in the trunk of my car, they buckled themselves in the back seat, and Auntie Gloria was in front with me.

As we were driving to my house, one of the girls asked what my favorite song was from their performance. This was my first clue the children had been nurtured in the art of polite conversation.

When we arrived home, they found their sleeping quarters and reappeared donned in pajamas.

As we sat at the dining room table for an evening snack, Auntie Gloria asked if we had any questions. She explained what their home life was like on the Watoto village campus in Africa. We learned there are opportunities for us to travel there for vacation or for work.

Auntie Gloria told us the children are given the opportunity to be on the tour just once in their lifetime. Most of the adult chaperones had also completed the tour as a child.

In order for the children to be prepared for their stay in the United States, they are required to go through six months of "intense training." Their training not only included the song and dance practice, but also how to conduct themselves while not on stage. Basically how to live your life.

I remember Gloria saying they believe politeness is really a "heart issue. It comes from the heart." Auntie Gloria placed her hand on her own heart while she was speaking. The children are taught how to be kind and considerate every moment of every day.

After all – life is simply one moment after another.

We learned that two of the girls were orphaned, and one still has her biological mother back home in the Watoto village.

They asked us about our own family, and they noticed photos around the house and on the refrigerator. I told them about my parents and my large family. I realized the difference. My parents lived to old age.

My husband and I both noticed how many times we heard the words "may I" and "thank you." We found ourselves thinking we could possibly travel with these children after all.

The next morning we had breakfast together before I drove them back to the church. The group gathered in the lobby for a few last laughs as we discussed how much fun we'd had. We gave them a gift of card games they would likely play on the bus, and we said our goodbyes to them.

Two years later, the Watoto Choir was again booked for an evening performance at the church. There was no hesitation on our part in letting the church know we would be a host family. Our upstairs bedrooms still looked good, so there was no underlying motive nudging us into opening our home.

The children would be here on a Tuesday. The weeks leading up to the performance were busy times for me. Our family would be coming in from out of town for my brother Stevie's 50th birthday party which we held at Edgerton's high school gymnasium.

We had invited the community and our large family to celebrate his birthday with us. And my ninety-two-year-old mother was looking forward to seeing her family and friends.

The 2019 Watoto Choir performance at the church was equally as inspiring as the show we'd seen two years prior. We noticed a little one in the choir. She was six years old and just as cute as a six-year-old should be. Her name was Ruthie, and after the show, we learned she would be staying at our house.

Our chaperone was twenty-five-year-old Auntie Joan, a soloist during the show. And a pretty ten-year-old, Shamira, would also be one of our guests.

While we were sitting at the dining room table for a bedtime snack, we asked Auntie Joan about their beautiful braids. She told us it takes a couple of hours to braid their hair, and it must be completed at least monthly.

The girls noticed the Watoto postcard from the 2017 performance was still on our refrigerator. They were able to identify their friends. We laughed that they knew they were staying at the same Ohio home a few of their friends had stayed in a couple of years ago.

After the girls headed upstairs and settled in for the night, my husband and I discussed how wonderful it is to be in their presence. Their manners and discipline were over-the-top. We jokingly asked if we could keep them. But we could see how beautifully they were already being taken care of.

In the morning, the girls were ready for the day before I was. Shamira noticed my wet hair and a blow-dryer in my hand while looking for an outlet to use. She asked me if she could blow-dry my hair for me.

So I sat on the family room floor near an outlet, and Shamira took the brush to task and dried my hair while Ruthie stood beside and watched.

I looked back at the email I had sent to my family the next day. I had told my mother and siblings I looked pretty goofy with the new hairstyle Shamira had created, but I combed my hair into place as I normally do and ended up with a good hair day.

The only mistake I made was not having had someone take a picture of Shamira drying my hair.

I had told Ruthie that my mother's name is Ruth, and there are many people who know her as "Ruthie." I asked her to guess how old my mom is. She didn't even come close, and I told her that Mom is ninety-two-and-a-half. Ruthie looked at me with a look of surprise and made us laugh.

There I sat, telling a six-year-old orphaned girl named Ruthie that my mother was still here with me. And I knew little Ruthie and Shamira were being raised in Uganda by people who were not their family members.

What I didn't know at the time I was telling them about my mother is that we would be in the emergency room with Mom seven days later.

Mom always told us she planned on leaving this earth as quickly as her sister-in-law, our Aunt Isabel, managed to do.

Our cousin Collene was with us at the hospital. She listened to the same ER doctor give the same diagnosis and prognosis to our mother that had been given to her mother – our Aunt Isabel.

I will probably never see Shamira and little Ruthie again, but I will always remember the braids. The politeness. The free hair-styling session. I'll remember the conversations about my mom and Ruthie's face when she learned my mother's age.

My mom and my Aunt Isabel not only raised their children and became grandmothers, they watched their children become grandparents. And their grandchildren become parents. Mom and Aunt Isabel knew what it was like to hold a great-grandchild in their arms.

The last big event my mom attended was Stevie's 50th birthday party. It was fun to watch her enjoy the day. As we were getting the tables set up and preparing for the celebration, her great-grandchildren pushed her in a wheelchair around the gym. She had as much fun as they.

It seemed Mom thought Stevie's party was her own party. She'd arranged for her own comfortable chair to be brought from her home, so she was able to remain seated as she greeted her friends and family.

We'd ordered a small pink corsage for her to wear with her favorite pink shirt. Many of her guests had noticed how beautifully the shirt and corsage went together.

Her elderly little hands had reached out and touched those who'd come to see Stevie as we celebrated his 50th birthday. None of us knew at the time that Mom was having her last conversation and last embrace with so many she'd loved and cared for.

I often remember that Auntie Gloria had told us the Watoto children go through six months of "intense training" before they are ready to tour with the choir.

I laugh at the thought of how magnificent the world would be if all the people of the land were required to go through six months of intense training. In kindness. We would learn the art of being kind. In every moment of every day. In every word. In every thought.

How wonderful it would be to receive a diploma identifying our achievements. Some of us already have an undergraduate degree in kindness and thoughtfulness. We could go on to earn an advanced degree – a Master of the Heart.

The children of the Watoto Choir were 7500 miles away from the place they called home. But they were not alone as they traveled through North America. Together they witnessed the beauty of the mountains and the rivers running through them. They saw trees in bloom as well as wildlife, bugs, and birds native to the land. They saw the beauty of life on this side of the earth.

My husband and I would like to do the same. To travel to their homeland and see the girls who've become young ladies. To see what's native to their land. To see what an ordinary life is like for them.

We'd have to reintroduce ourselves. After all, that's the polite thing to do. And we'd once again hear their beautiful little voices as they call us by name – Auntie Marlene and Uncle Pat.

How wonderful it is to spend time with friends who live nearby, as well as those who happen to live on the other side of the world. There's so much to learn. So much to understand. So many ways to earn our degree in kindness. As we live in joy. In each brand new day. In our own rebirth.

Members of the 2019 Watoto Village Children's Choir on stage at St. Paul's Church in Montpelier, Ohio.

Watoto Village is a safe place where orphaned children can truly experience the love of a family. Their story can be found at www.watoto.com.

"GRANDMA, YOU ALREADY AM OLD!"

Sleep Tight

When my grandchildren stay overnight at my house, at the end of the day I hear them say one of my favorite words: "Nighty-night."

The Urban Dictionary is an online site I visit every so often to make sure the meaning of certain words hasn't changed. It's saved me more than a few times. The younger generation knows the modern-day meaning of old catchphrases.

Thankfully, "nighty-night" and "sleep tight" still mean we are letting someone know, in a cute way, to sleep well.

In today's world, our friends can send a quick text message to wish us a good night. Sometimes there's a sleep emoji and a picture of the moon within the text. Although it's an electronic message, our minds still hear their voice as we read it, and we know we're in their thoughts.

Several years ago, a friend of mine went through major surgery. She told me she actually "felt" the prayers. I can't think of a better place to be than in someone's thoughts and prayers.

My mother taught my siblings and me to pray together as a family. If you were to ask a brother or sister of mine about our nighttime prayers, you'd see a smile as they recount the story.

I never asked my parents if their families had prayed together as they were growing up. Funny the questions we have after they are gone.

All of us know the feeling of being so tired we fall asleep soon after we crawl into bed. We also know there are times when the problems of the day dance in our heads and make falling asleep a task that's not so easy.

As we grow up and grow old, our prayers change. Each season of life brings new reasons to be grateful. We end up with friends who've stayed nearby and friends who've moved away. Friends who've challenged us. Who've lifted us up. Who didn't let us play small.

We're left with fond memories of the times we'd spent together. And our prayers, much like words from a love song, can overwhelm us. With gratitude. If we let them.

Nighty-Night

Now I lay me down to sleep.
I wonder what I'm supposed to think.

I tell my mind it would be best
to please agree on needed rest!

I feel a peace flood over me
as I dream of all I have today.

I pray my friends and family
can feel the love I'm sending.

So many I cherish:

The person who became my spouse.
My children and their children.
Grandma and Grandpa – in my thoughts since long ago.
Mom and Dad too.

Brothers and sisters. In-laws and outlaws.
Cousins, so many.

My aunts and uncles
and the older generation
with "Great" before their names.

My nieces and nephews
with their newest additions –
another generation of Greats.

I don't know what I'd do without my friends.
I wouldn't be me if I didn't have them.
Those who text
Those who call
Those I met on my Facebook wall.

My friends who get together
for campfires and s'mores.

Games to play and foot races to race.
Bubbles to blow and dodge balls to throw.

Memories of good times together.
Gladness in knowing there will be more.

Never will we hear a "Nighty-night"
from someone we don't know.

Just like their hugs. Just like their kisses.
And their sloppy Xs and Os.

When they tell us to sleep tight
and wish for us sweet dreams

How wonderful it is to know –
it's really love they're sending.

Postscript

Who doesn't stick around for the P.S.? That's where all the fun is. After all, most of us have skipped to the bottom of a note and read the P.S. first. It's just too tempting.

So I'll use this postscript to thank those who've read my books, newspaper columns, and blog stories. Thanks for sticking around.

Thanks also for sharing your thoughts. The comments on social media are fun to read, and I've felt encouraged. My gratitude journal is one I didn't write. It's a journal full of letters, notes, and emails. Written by others. It doesn't get any better than that.

Putting our papers, cards, and memorabilia we've collected along the way into one special book is like taking time to build a beautiful perennial garden. It'll take a little work, but it's the fun kind of work.

Just as a garden provides a place for flowers to bloom once again, a gratitude journal does the same with words. Those old Xs and Os will startle us if we're not ready for them. There they are, jumping off the page. Their meaning coming to life once more.

Reading words that'd been penned to us so many years ago is a way of jump-starting the heart. A way of reminding us of times gone by. We see how riveting our life has been. And how the suspense and drama were simply a part of the life we were meant to live.

We'll come to the end of our big book of things that made us happy and notice there are blank pages waiting to be filled. And we'll be inspired. There's more living to do. More paths to discover. More Xs and Os to add to our collection.

All the best,

Marlene Oxender

P.S. XOXO

Now the end again.

My fourth book, *Remember That Time*, is next in the queue and is a compilation of stories about growing up in a small town in Ohio.

If you've enjoyed this book, as well as *Picket Fences* and *Stevie*, a review on Amazon would be greatly appreciated. Just locate the books on the Amazon website. Under "Review this product," click on the "Write a customer review" link.

Written reviews are needed, appreciated, and downright coveted by writers. Thank you for taking a few minutes to share your thoughts with others. A written review is truly a gift to an author.

Picket Fences

A collection of personal stories inspired by
the memorabilia Marlene discovered in her parents' estate.

Marlene and her ten siblings grew up in a small town in rural Ohio. Her parents purchased their family home in 1947 and lived there for over seventy years.

It was a time when families spent Sundays together. There were sleepovers. Barns to play in. Farms to explore. Ponds to fish in. Games to play.

When Marlene began sorting through her mother's boxes of newspaper clippings, she also discovered decades-old greeting cards, letters, grade cards, scrapbooks, and never-before-seen photos from their childhood. The family came to refer to their mother's saved cardboard boxes as "time capsules."

Picket Fences is the first volume in the *Picket Fences American Family Series* and is available on Amazon.

Stevie

Marlene's second book is a collection of personal stories written about her younger brother, Steven Kimpel.

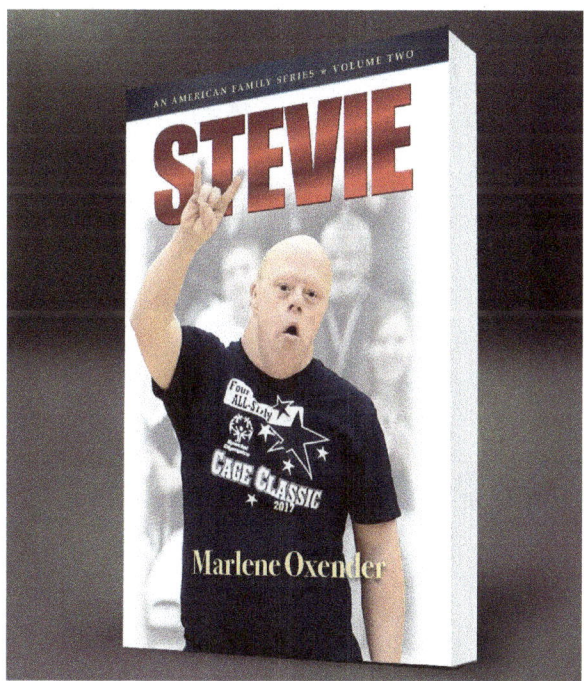

Marlene was one of ten siblings who learned, back in 1969, that their youngest brother was born with Down syndrome.

At the time of Stevie's birth, his parents were told he would not live past the age of five. They were told their newborn son would not be accepted by his older siblings nor by friends and extended family.

Stevie's parents chose to take him home and raise him with the rest of their children. They quickly learned that the opposite of what they were told was true. Stevie was surrounded by family and friends who not only accepted him, they loved him. They helped care for him.

Stevie proved to the world that his fifty-four-year walk on earth would be a joyful one. Stevie taught us how to celebrate the little things.

Stevie is the second volume in the *Picket Fences American Family Series* and is available on Amazon.

www.ingramcontent.com/pod-product-compliance
Lightning Source LLC
Chambersburg PA
CBHW071225090426
42736CB00014B/2974